Bernadette Cuxart

ART Painting with...

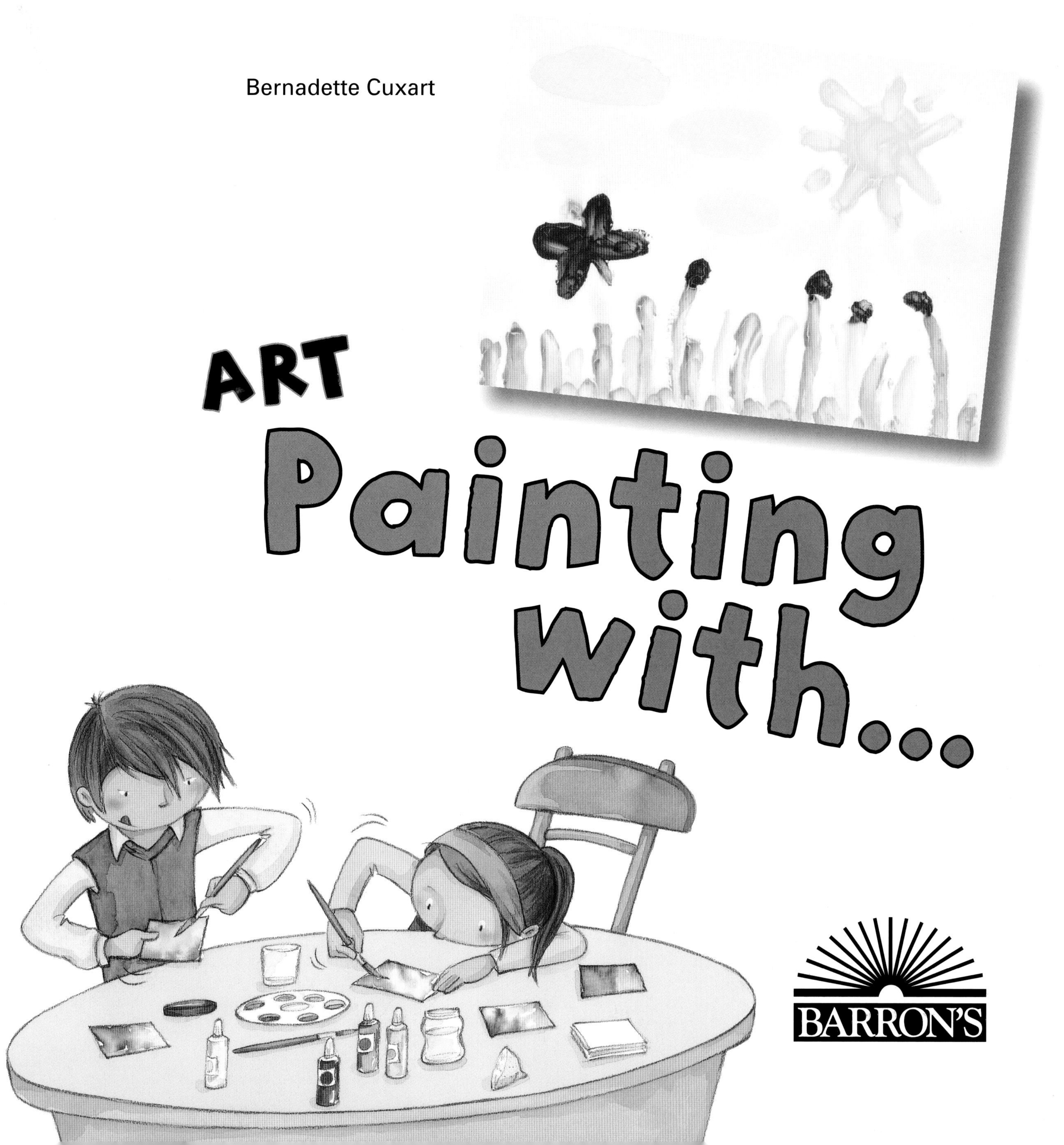

CONT

eNTS

Surely you know a few water games you enjoy in the summer—but none as artistic as the one we're going to show you now!

QUICK DRAWINGS with water

MATERIALS: A cup of water, thick paintbrushes, water toys (water guns, water shooters, etc.), and a smooth, flat floor.

1 Find a cup and fill it with water.

2 Prepare a few "tools" that you can use to paint with water: different-sized paintbrushes, water guns, water shooters, a roller, cardboard tubes... It is easy to find lots of things you can use!

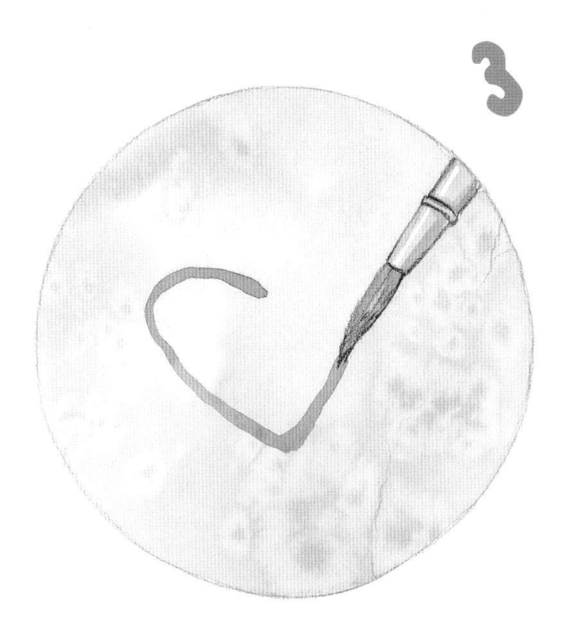

3 Look for an outdoor surface where you can paint with water (a terrace, an outdoor court...). Begin by wetting a paintbrush in the water, and then start painting!

4 Try to make circles with a tube and then experiment with all the other things you have.

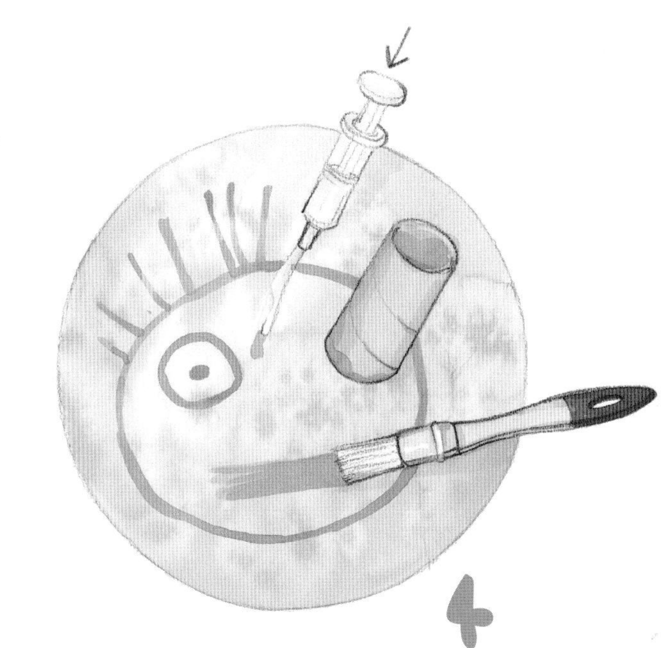

On sunny days, your drawings aren't going to last very long, maybe just a few minutes or even seconds. So... start all over again! Doesn't it seem magical?

LIZARDS with water-soluble dyes and salt

If you add textures to the animals you draw, they will look even more life-like!

MATERIALS: Salt, water-soluble dyes, white construction paper, a mixing palette, paintbrushes, a graphite pencil, a colored pencil or a black wax pencil, and a cup of water.

1 Draw an animal that has rough or textured skin, such as an elephant, a dragon, a dinosaur, or a lizard. Trace over the outline heavily with a colored or black wax pencil.

2 On the color palette, prepare the colored dyes you want to use, and paint the different parts of the animals. You can mix the different colors right on the paper as long as the dye is still wet.

3 While the colored dye is still wet, sprinkle it with a bit of salt. As it dries, you'll see how the dye gathers wherever the salt is, making a really great texture.

You can see the kinds of textures you can get by mixing water-soluble dyes and salt. Think about what else you can use it for...

4 When your artwork is totally dry, you can remove the excess salt. First shake the construction paper so the loose salt falls off, and then remove the rest by rubbing it with your fingers.

CREATIONS with coffee

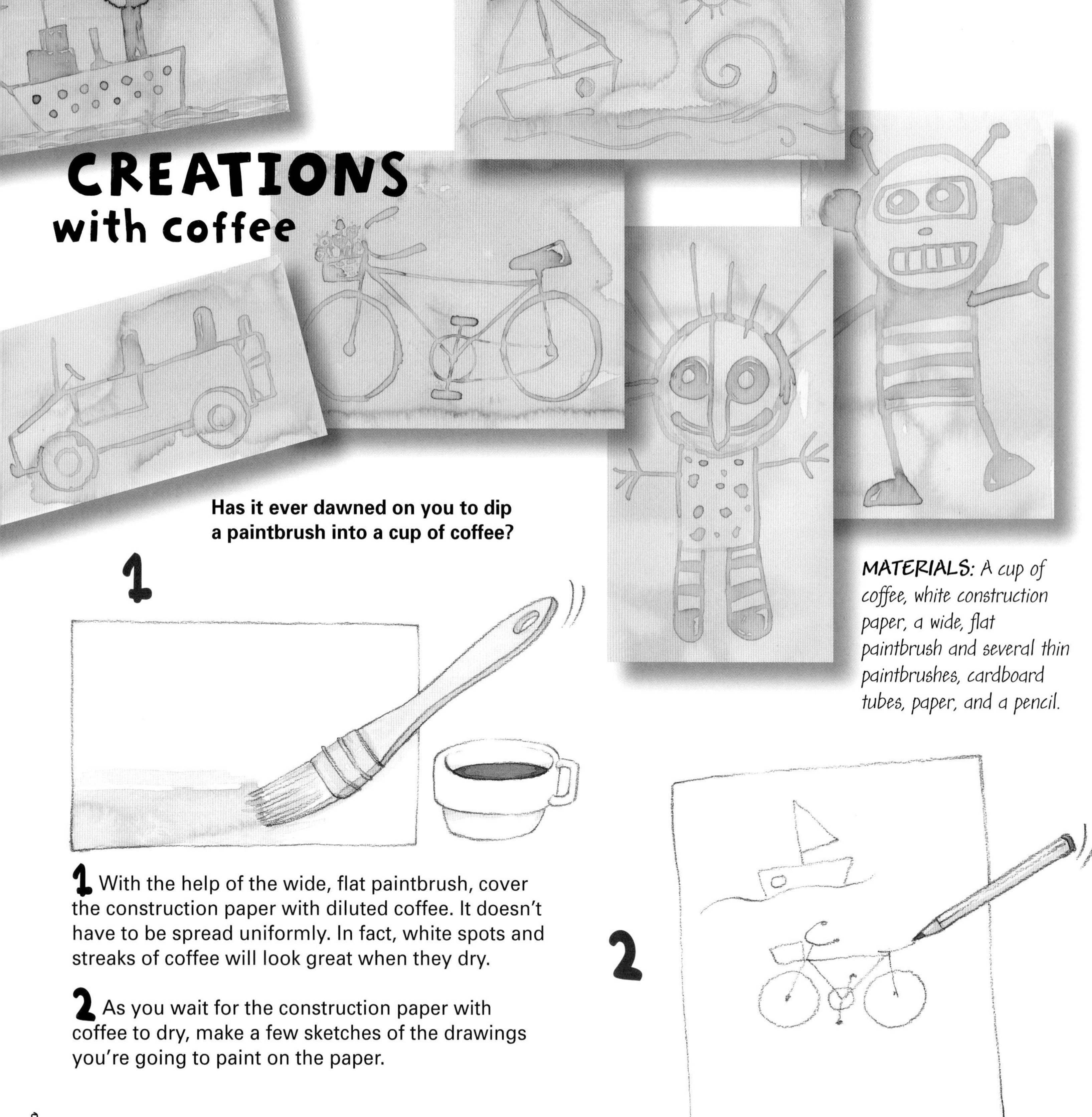

Has it ever dawned on you to dip a paintbrush into a cup of coffee?

MATERIALS: A cup of coffee, white construction paper, a wide, flat paintbrush and several thin paintbrushes, cardboard tubes, paper, and a pencil.

1 With the help of the wide, flat paintbrush, cover the construction paper with diluted coffee. It doesn't have to be spread uniformly. In fact, white spots and streaks of coffee will look great when they dry.

2 As you wait for the construction paper with coffee to dry, make a few sketches of the drawings you're going to paint on the paper.

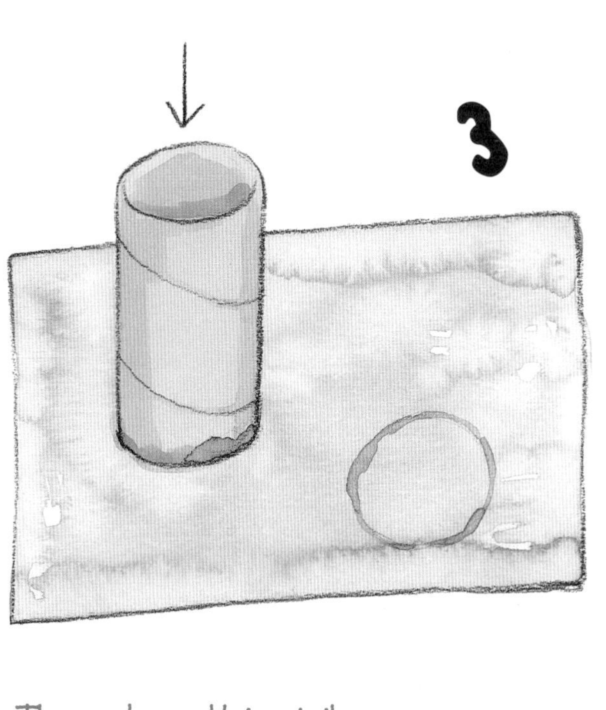

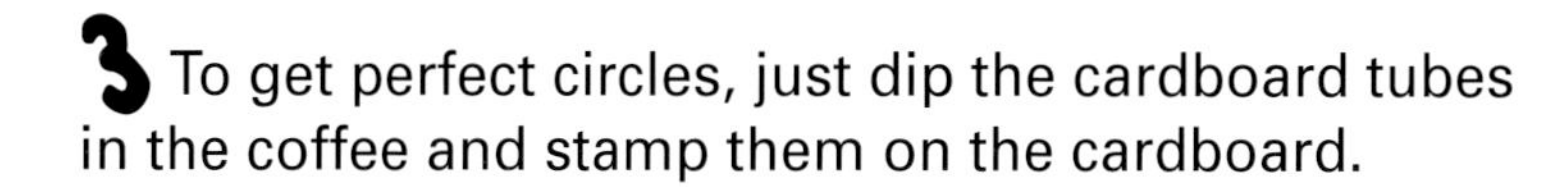

3 To get perfect circles, just dip the cardboard tubes in the coffee and stamp them on the cardboard.

4 Use the coffee as if it were paint: dip your paintbrushes in it and paint whatever you want right on the paper.

The end result is similar to a watercolor, in beautiful, natural sepia tones.

NIGHTTIME

with crayons and paint

Think about colors that stand out on nighttime black. What will you dream of?

1 Paint the construction paper with crayons, creating a mosaic of many different colors. Be sure not to leave any white spaces!

MATERIALS:
White construction paper, crayons, a small dish, dishwashing liquid, black acrylic paint, a thick paintbrush, toothpicks, glossy paper, and scissors.

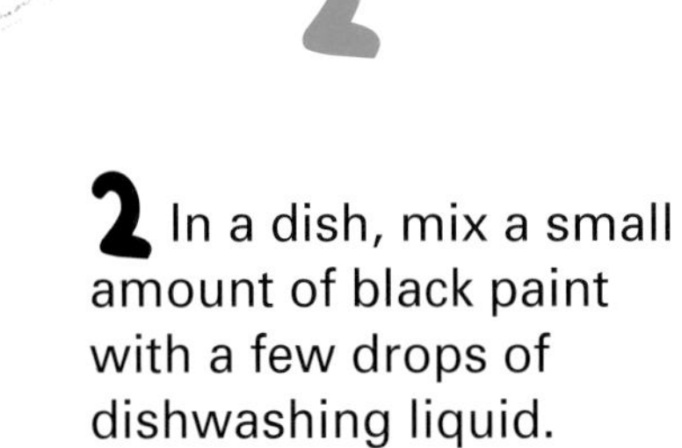

2 In a dish, mix a small amount of black paint with a few drops of dishwashing liquid.

3 Using a paintbrush, cover the entire construction paper with the black paint mixture.

4 Cut off the tip of a toothpick so it is not too sharp, and use it to make drawings over the painted paper. You'll see how the colors show through under the lines you draw!

Another possibility is covering a piece of colored glossy paper directly with the black paint mixture. Look at the example of the airplane flying in the night sky on the opposite page—it's amazing, isn't it?

We're going to show you another use for shaving foam that we bet you've never imagined...

RELIEFS with shaving foam

MATERIALS: Little plastic ziplock bags, shaving foam, white glue, liquid paint (dye) or coloring, scissors, colored construction paper, colored paper, colored markers or pencils, a glue stick, and decorative items (beads, sprigs, etc.).

1 To make a white relief painting, put equal parts of shaving foam and white glue in a ziplock bag. If you want to make a colored painting, just add a few drops of dye or liquid paint. The brightness of the color will depend on the amount of dye or paint you add.

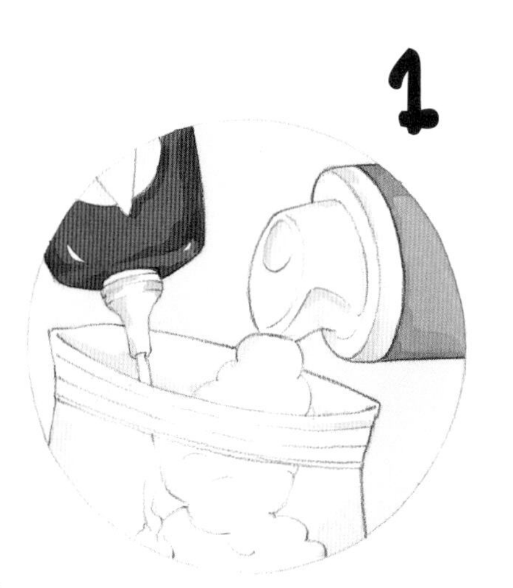

2 Then push the contents of the bag to the bottom with your fingers, let out a bit of air and zip the bag closed. Mix the contents well using your fingers until the color is uniform. Make a tiny cut in the corner of the bag.

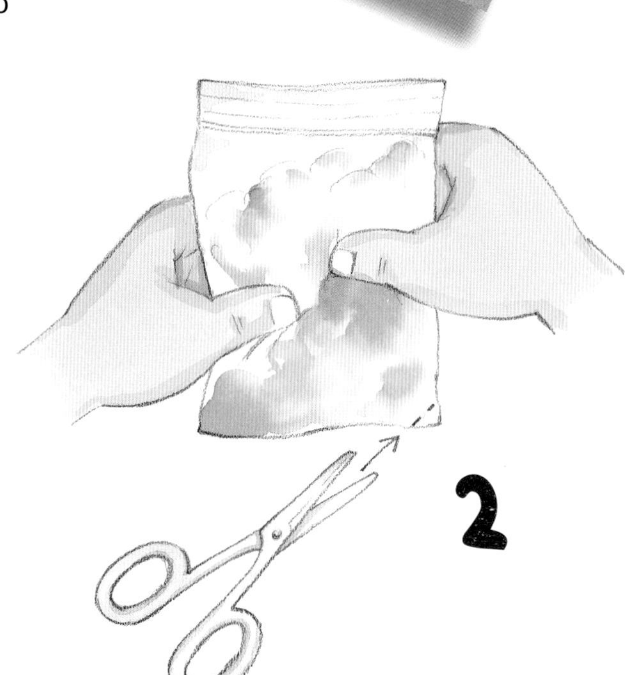

3 Plan your painting. Before you apply the mixture, color or glue on the parts that are going to be flat.

4 And now comes the fun part! Press on the bag using your hands to make the paint ooze out of the little opening in the corner, like a pastry sleeve. Use this paint mixture to cover all the parts that you want to stick out in relief. Let it dry.

Before the paint dries, you can add beads, tiny sprigs, or anything else you can think of.

Have you ever used invisible ink? You don't need to go to a science lab to make it… just look in your fridge!

SECRETS

with milk

MATERIALS: A cup, milk, a paintbrush, white paper, and an iron.

1 Think about who you'd like to send a secret message to… and what you'd like to say.

2 Pour a small amount of milk into a glass.

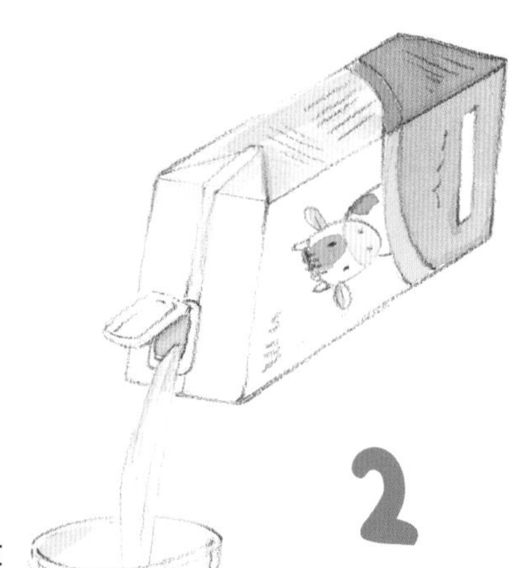

3 Dip your paintbrush into the milk and write or draw on the paper. You have to know what you want to do beforehand because you can't see the white milk on white paper. That's what makes it fun!

4 To see what you have drawn or written, you need to iron the paper. Ask an adult to do this for you, and you'll see how your brushstrokes gradually appear in a brownish tone.

So what do you think about this original way to send secret messages? It also works by replacing milk with squeezed lemon juice.

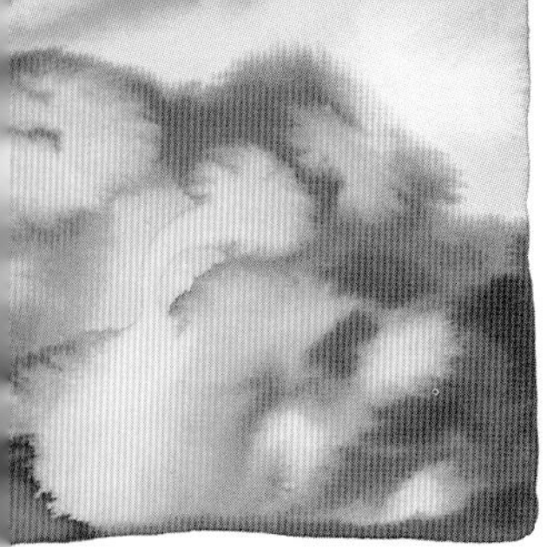

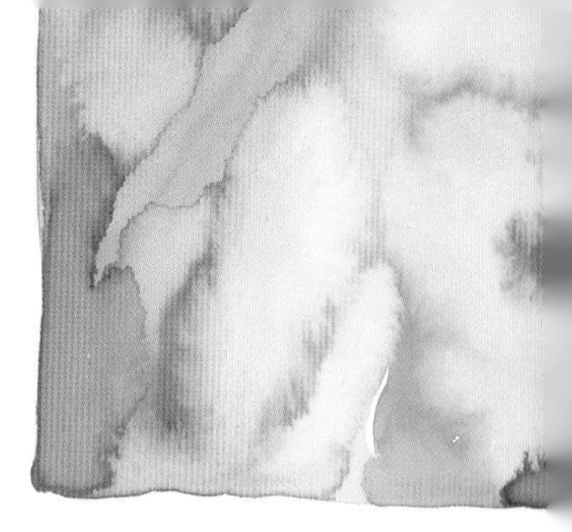

MATERIALS: Water-soluble dyes, a mixing palette, paintbrushes, half a lemon, a juicer, a cup, a cup of water, white construction paper, and scissors.

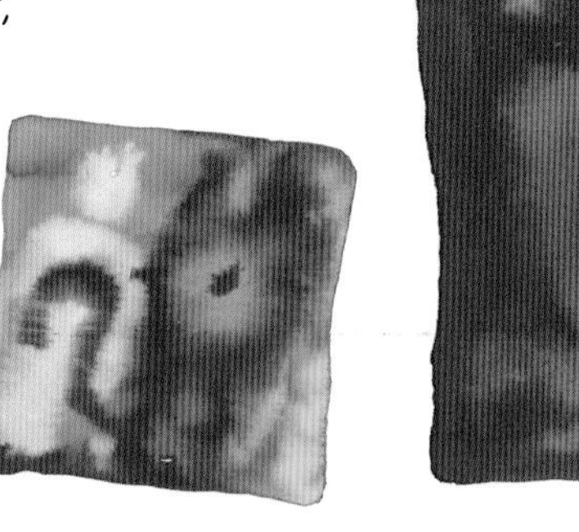
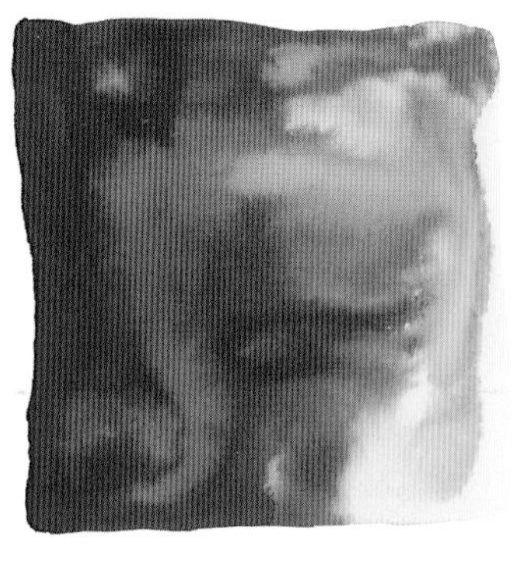
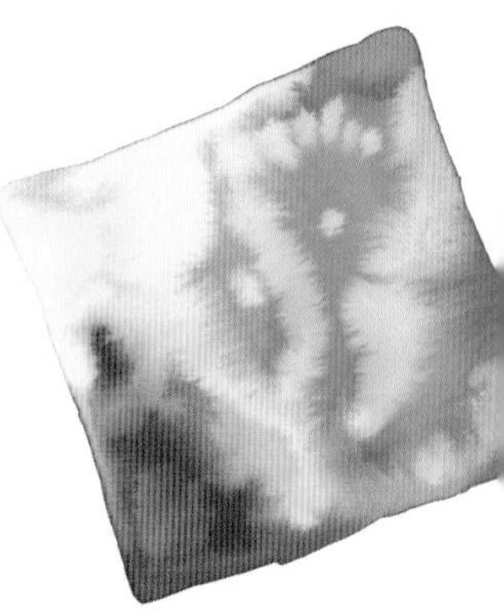

CARDS with water-soluble dyes and lemon

Lemon juice reacts when it touches the paint and you never know how it's going to turn out… It's so exciting!

1 Squeeze the juice from half a lemon and pour it into a cup.

2 Prepare everything you need: the juice, a cup of water, little pieces of construction paper, and the dye. Put the colors you like on the palette and mix them. Now that you've started, you've got to work quickly!

3
3 Dip the paintbrush into a color and make a mark on the cardboard. Keep marking it with other colors, mixing them together. Keep dipping the brush in the water, too, so that the paint stays wet and the colors mix together.
4 Then, while the paint is still wet, dip the brush into the lemon juice and paint it over the color. You'll see how beautiful colorful streaks form. Move the cardboard around so that the trails slide around. Let it dry.
4
If the shapes on the construction paper look like something in particular, you can give it a few finishing touches with markers.

A LITTLE HOUSE with modeling clay

MATERIALS:
Cardboard, modeling clay, a pencil, paints, a dish, a paintbrush, varnish or transparent nail polish, marker tops, straws, and toothpicks.

Drawings in relief always make you want to touch them, don't they?

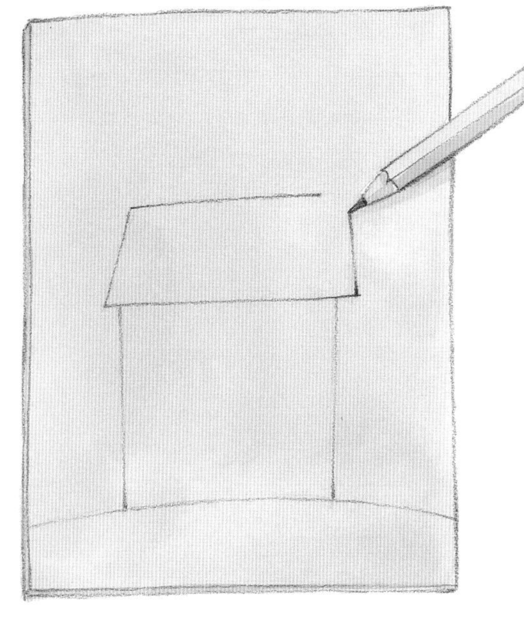

1 Make a simple drawing on a rectangular piece of cardboard.

2 Fill the spaces in your drawing with little balls of modeling clay that you press together. Press them with your fingers until they are nice and smooth.

4 For a better finish, paint the areas of the cardboard that are not covered with clay. Finally, varnish the clay to protect it.

3 Once you've got the main areas of your drawing covered with clay, it's time for the details and the textures using anything you've got on hand. You can trace lines with a toothpick to make the clay look like wood, or you simulate roof tiles by pressing the top of a marker at a slight angle, etc.

The paint will also help you to hide the stains that modeling clay often leaves on cardboard.

A MERMAID with glitter

Glitter works wonders to give invitations and greeting cards a festive touch.

MATERIALS: *Construction paper, glitter, glue, a paintbrush, a pencil, colored pencils, and newspaper.*

1 Make a pencil drawing on the construction paper. Think about something that sparkles... what comes to mind?

2 Fill it in with lots of colors, except for the parts that you want to sparkle.

3 With the help of the paintbrush, apply glue to the areas that should be shiny, and then quickly sprinkle a good amount of glitter onto the glue before it dries. Do this over the newspaper so that later you can collect the glitter that doesn't stick.

4 Wait a few minutes and then shake the drawing over the newspaper to remove the extra glitter.

You can put the glitter that didn't stick to your drawing back in the tube and use it another day.

MATERIALS: *Water, plastic cups or bowls, paper, straws, paints, liquid dish soap, colored and tissue paper, scissors, and a glue stick.*

1 In a bowl or cup, mix water with paint and a few drops of dish soap. Put enough paint to stain the mixture the color you want.

2 Blow through a straw until bubbles are overflowing from the bowl or cup.

3 Put a piece of paper over the bubbles, and you'll see how the bubbles color the paper. Repeat steps 2 and 3 until you fill your piece of paper with paint bubbles.

4 Finish your artwork with other items, like little pieces of tissue paper. In our drawing we added green leaves, since our bubbles looked like hydrangeas, don't you think?

Another idea: if you make blue bubbles, you can finish your artwork with colorful little fish.

A PAINTING with chalk and salt

Once you've mastered this technique, you'll be able to create amazing landscapes!

1 The first step is to dye the salt. Place it on a sheet of paper and rub it with the colored chalk. Make several little piles of different-colored salt.

MATERIALS: Rock salt, colored chalk, a piece of glass, thick cardboard, scissors that can cut cardboard, regular and two-sided cellophane tape, and sheets of paper.

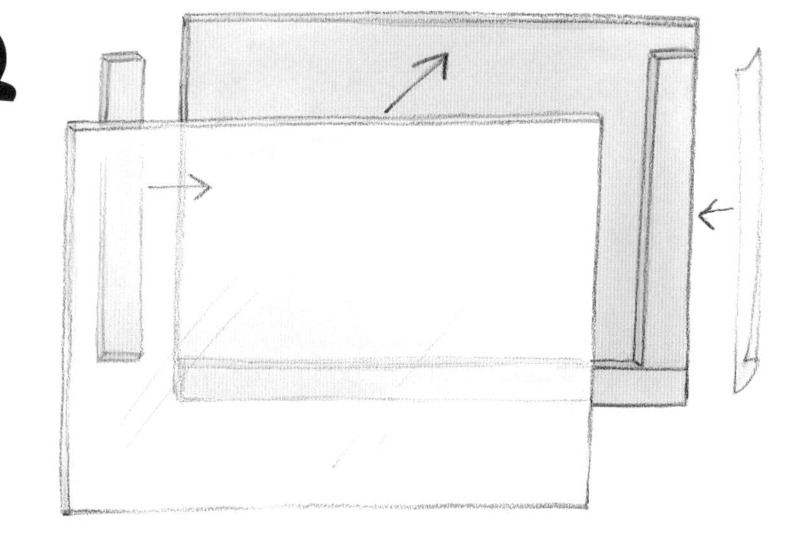

2 Cut a piece of cardboard the same size as the piece of glass, along with four $^1/_2$ in. ($1^1/_2$ cm) cardboard strips: two the same length as the glass and another two the same height as the glass minus $1^1/_4$ in. (3 cm). Using two-sided cellophane tape, glue the strips to the cardboard like an inner frame, and put the glass on top. Attach the bottom and two side strips with cellophane tape.

3 Now fold the sheet of paper with the little piles of colored salt, and carefully place the end into the upper opening between the glass and the cardboard. Let the salt fall into the opening, making layers of colors.

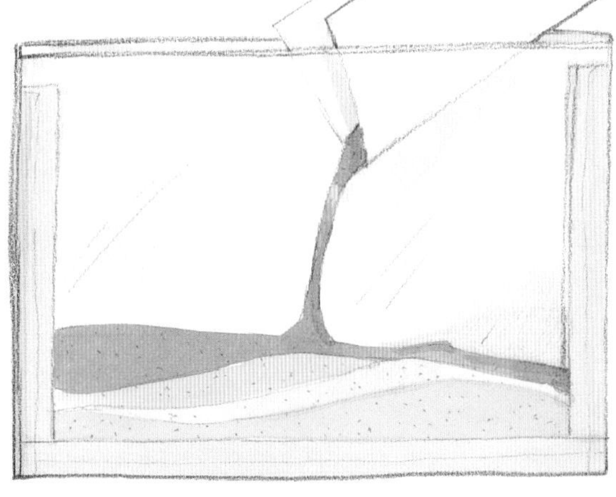

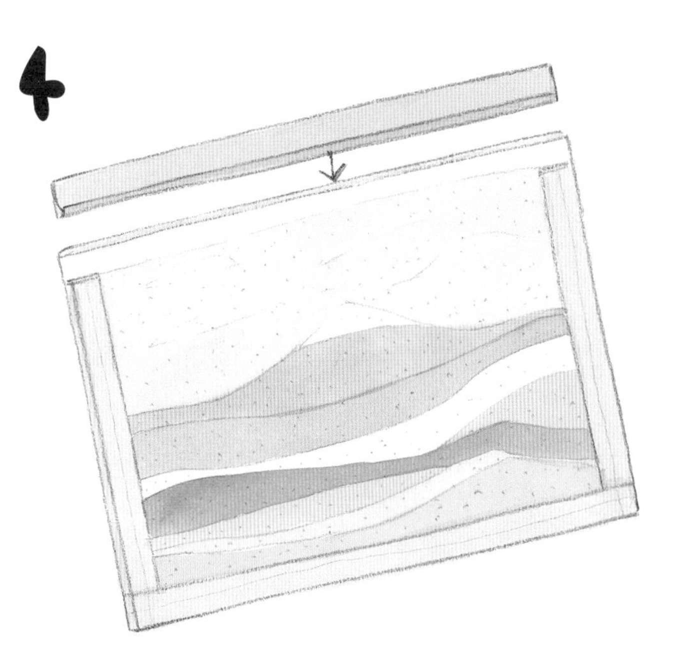

4 When it is completely full of salt and only 1/2 in. (1 1/2 cm) of empty space remains at the top, place the last cardboard strip and attach it with tape. Make sure that there are no holes where the salt can escape.

Small glass jars filled with layers of colored salt are also beautiful!

This is a very fun, relaxing art project!

SURPRISES with ink and water

MATERIALS: *Styrofoam tray, water, India ink, a fine paintbrush, tongs, sheets of paper, and newspaper.*

1

1 Put a bit of water in the tray (approximately $^1/_2$ in. deep) and leave on a flat surface.

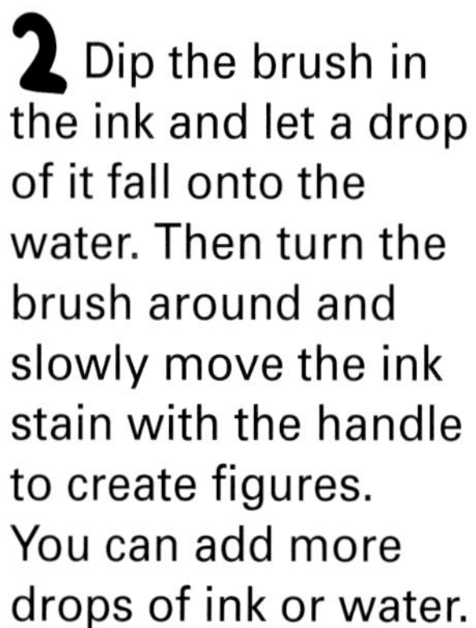

2

2 Dip the brush in the ink and let a drop of it fall onto the water. Then turn the brush around and slowly move the ink stain with the handle to create figures. You can add more drops of ink or water.

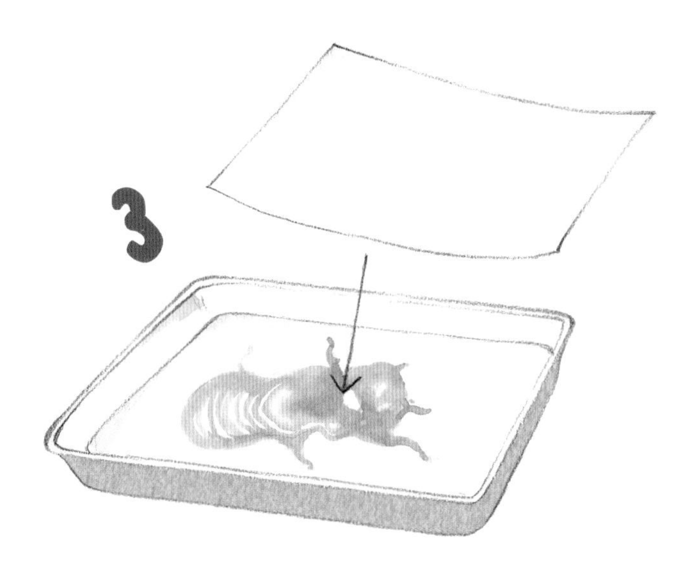

3 When you like the shape that the ink is making, carefully place a piece of paper on the surface of the water. In just a few seconds the paper will absorb the ink and the water.

4 When the paper begins to curl up, remove it with the tongs. Let it dry face up on the newspaper.

Keep trying and you'll realize that no two ink stains are the same. You'll no doubt create terrifying monsters you're sure to love!

This technique is ideal for painting landscapes quickly and easily.

MATERIALS: Thick white paper or construction paper, crayons, watercolors, water, and paintbrushes.

LANDSCAPES with crayons and watercolors

1 Is it a beautiful day today? If so, gather everything you need and head outside to paint! You can carry the water in a closed jar.

2 Look at the landscape and plan what you want to paint. You can make a snowy landscape using white crayons. Flowers also look pretty when drawn with crayons. Or maybe a sunset with black crayons.

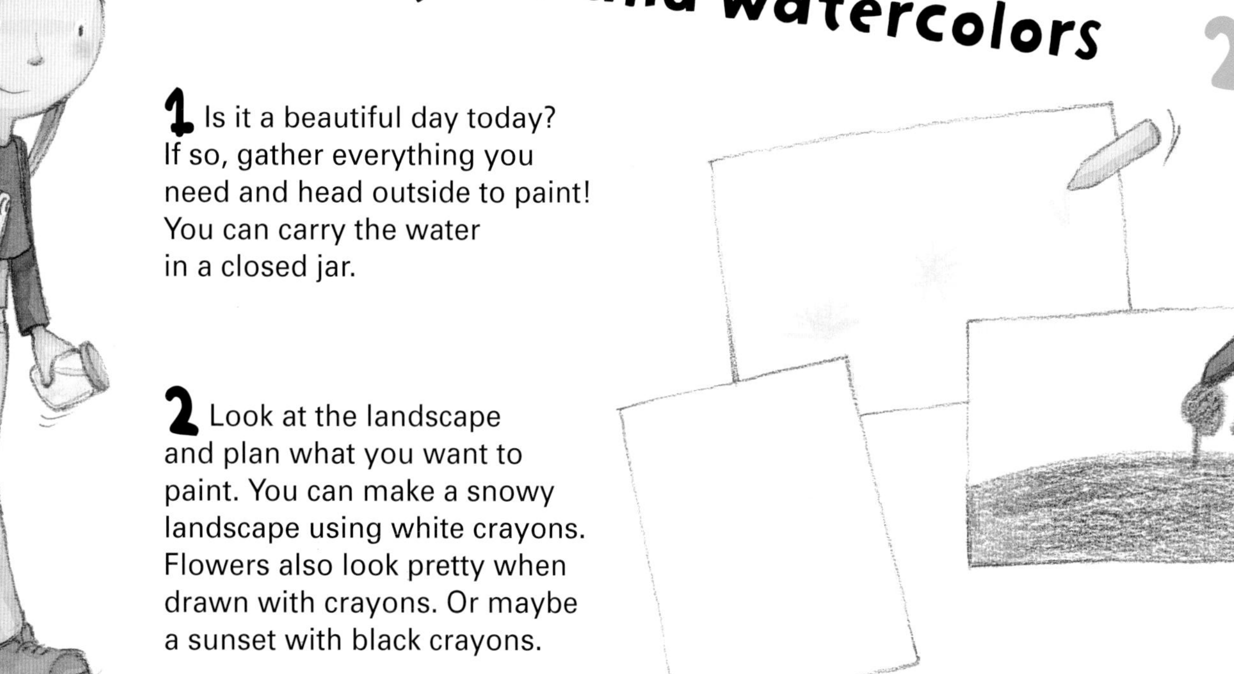

4 Experiment with mixing colors while the paper is still wet. You'll get really beautiful effects in your skies, for example.

3 The wax of the crayons repels liquids like watercolors, so everything that you draw or color with crayons should stay the same color, but you can fill in the spaces you have left empty with the watercolors of your choice.

Painting landscapes outdoors is a fascinating experience. You've got to try it!

IMAGINATION with homemade edible finger paint

If you want to paint but you don't have any paint left, no problem! You can make it yourself!

MATERIALS: Corn starch, cold and hot water, a pot to boil water on the stove, food coloring, construction paper, glass jars, and a spoon.

1 Mix two parts cold water to one part corn starch. If you add a drop of food coloring to the mix, you will get a pasty paint that can be applied using a paintbrush. But for our purposes don't add color yet and instead continue the process.

2 For thicker paint, add two more parts of water to the previous mixture and boil it briefly on the stove until it thickens (keep stirring it to prevent it from getting lumpy). Let it cool.

3 Divide the paste into different jars so you can make different colors. Add drops of food coloring to each jar and mix well using a spoon. And now you've got paint that is ready to use!

4 Moisten your index finger in the paints and combine the colors you've prepared. When you finish painting, you can cover the jars and save the paint in the fridge for a few days.

This paint is ideal for little children, although it shouldn't take the place of their afternoon snack, of course...!

Did you know that blackboards don't have to be black, or green?

MATERIALS: Acrylic paint, chalk powder, hot water, coarse and fine sandpaper, pieces of wood, a thick, soft paintbrush, a cup for mixing, and a measuring cup.

SIGNS with blackboard paint

1 Look for little pieces of wood that you can use for this project (fruit boxes, for example). Sand them down with the coarse sandpaper.

2 Prepare the paint in a cup, mixing all the ingredients well in the following proportions: three parts paint, two parts chalk powder, and one part hot water.

3 Paint the entire surface of the wood, trying to keep it totally uniform. Let it dry.

4 Once the wood is dry, smooth it using fine-grained sandpaper moistened in water. Wait until it dries, and then apply a second layer of paint. If needed, repeat the process a third time. The surface should be as smooth as a blackboard so you can write on it with chalk.

You can also apply this paint on furniture or walls, and if so you'll have a home full of blackboards where you can draw or write messages!

You can get a watercolor effect using other materials, such as marker ink diluted in water.

FLOWERS with marker water

MATERIALS: Markers (some working and others dried out), little cups, white paper, a piece of construction paper, a clothespin, a thick paintbrush, newspaper, regular and two-sided cellophane tape, a compass, and skewers.

1 The first step is to make "marker water" by soaking the tips of one or several dried out markers. As the water gradually colors, cut out different-sized circles and flowers out of white paper.

2 Using the markers that still work, paint concentric borders in several colors on your cut-outs, and then fold them in half three times.

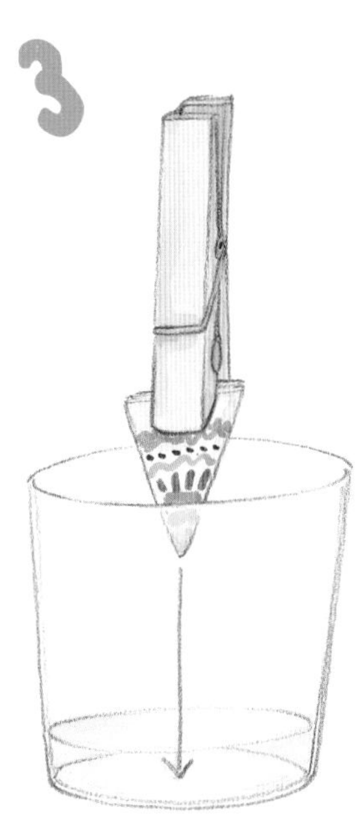

3 Holding a cut-out with the clothespin, place it tip down in a glass with a bit of water that reaches halfway up. You'll see how the colors gradually blend and creep up the paper. Dry it, open it carefully and place it on newspaper to dry.

4 In the meantime, you can prepare a background on a piece of construction paper. Draw stems with a marker and color it all with the "marker water" you have made. Once dried, you can now stick the flowers onto the stems using two-sided cellophane tape.

4

Here's another idea: paint some skewers green and use a bit of tape to attach them to the back of your flowers like stems.

First edition for North America published in 2015 by
Barron's Educational Series, Inc.
Original title of the book in Catalan: *L'art de pintar amb materials del dia a dia*

c/Castell, 38; Teià(0829) Barcelona, Spain (World Rights)
Tel: 93 540 13 53
E-mail: *info@mercedesros.com*
Website: *www.mercedesros.com*
Author and illustrator: Bernadette Cuxart

ISBN: 978-1-4380-0654-3
Library of Congress Control No.: 2014949908

All inquiries should be addressed to:
Barron's Educational Series, Inc.
250 Wireless Boulevard
Hauppauge, NY 11788
www.barronseduc.com

Printed in China
9 8 7 6 5 4 3 2 1

Date of Manufacture: January 2015
Place of Manufacture: L. REX PRINTING COMPANY LIMITED, Dongguan City, Guangdong, China